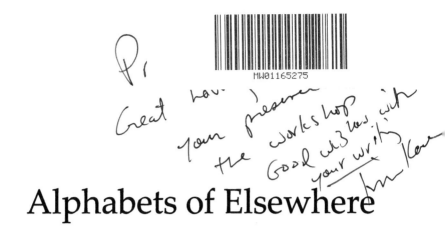

Alphabets of Elsewhere

Tim Keane

Independent Innovative International

Published by Cinnamon Press
Meirion House
Glan yr afon
Tanygrisiau
Blaenau Ffestiniog
Gwynedd LL41 3SU
www.cinnamonpress.com

The right of Tim Keane to be identified as author of this work has been asserted by him in accordance with the Copyright, Designs and Patent Act, 1988. © 2007 Tim Keane.

ISBN 978-1-905614-38-7
British Library Cataloguing in Publication Data. A CIP record for this book can be obtained from the British Library

All rights reserved. No part of this publication may be reproduced, stored in a retrieval system, or transmitted in any form or by any means, electronic, mechanical, photocopying, recording or otherwise without either the prior written permission of the publishers. This book may not be lent, hired out, resold or otherwise disposed of by way of trade in any form of binding or cover other than that in which it is published, without the prior consent of the publishers.

Designed and typeset in Palatino by Cinnamon Press. Cover design Mike Fortune-Wood from original artwork 'flapper' by Jaimie Duplas courtesy of dreamstime.com

Acknowledgements: Most of the poems in this book originally appeared in print and online venues, for which the author is grateful. In the US: *American Writing, Apostrophe: USBC Journal of the Arts, Big Bridge, Denver Quarterly, The Disquieting Muses Review, Free Verse, The Hampden-Sydney Poetry Review, Icon, International Poetry Review, Mudlark, Shenandoah, Sierra Nevada College Review, Potomac Review, Snow Monkey, , Sou'wester, Starfish Poetry, XCP: Cross-Cultural Poetics,* and *Wisconsin Review.* In the UK: *Aesthetica Magazine, Chimera, Great Works, Modern Painters, Stride Magazine, Zafusy, Pennine Platform,* and *Poetry Scotland.* In Singapore: *Quarterly Literary Review Singapore* and *Softblow.*

Contents

If the sea-water did not rise into the sky,
where would the garden get its life?

Rumi

Alphabets of Elsewhere

Painting Daybreak

come, wake, I'm painting daybreak:
draping gauze on tufted hedges
sketching yellow hills, promises,
Chinese radicals, drawing silk-screens,
scribbling odes ('Rose-Licked Gardens',
'The Drowsy Tortoise') living, charged,
like the novel, *Monkey*, a demon-charmer,
speeding slowly, letting life go,
a scrolling ink-soaked masterwork —
over Eastern trees of the studio,
answering rejects with erotic wishes —
I try out these cinctured tones,
this palette's a bounty — predawn,
pink-fleck clouds, perpetual Easters,
here, alive means livid, Jean Genet,
in love with the white-gloved acrobats
mocking Colleges of Category-Maids,
embarrassing your assistant-managing
nothings-in-chief: dropping pages, sedatives
& special issues, reminders, remainders.

I accept the brush, there's no obedience
no careful stillness, no staid insistence,
this here's now an everywhere, lingua,
ling chih, words burning ceiling to sun,
as yellows flow, fish-rich & streaming
strings of a land & air overture here
on seven I can see – 'Unmarried Time',
inventing lines to teach truer psalms–
thought is, finally, feeling, the sky is
another face of love & the sea answers
air in tides, tone & lines, verse circles,
abandons gray duty & dances, is undone,
stanzas swim in sins, desire embodies colors
colors con-fused to beauty, ignite the season's
dangerous return, annihilating fires of the satyr's reign.

Bronx River Rite

remember, kiddies when '99 was
coming like fat Christmas? now
a stale gin, millennial hangover
persists in been-there, done-that
dictions, in screen-distractions
in credit treats, corporate tricks
& digital, rack rent thieving.

America's air has broken its
compact with the sovereign body.

Hungry eyes & ears are left wanting.

Far from ruined cities, I live to see
the trees & long to forget the forest.

I'm Basho of the 'burbs
free of chic-ironies
& the canon's shots.

I shred topical scriptures
& I write of gods
with mixed success.

One will never know
the night for all along
one is the night.

I try open admissions–

I'm the night I know, I live
at a train line where gum trees grow,
against colorful rubbish, branching
over rusty scab-wire & green-beds
to where the Bronx River keeps
itself alive along the weedy overgrowth
where crickets' chirr sings to late summer
after lovers have gone & the poet's mornings rise
beyond the season's slow receding.

Waving Surface of Spring Flood

water waves on the silkscreen
draw down harmonies waxing
waning: ink-squibs fade in fog
seen so well until new seeing
moves me into myself, off, out
into a strange flux & fluid life
of fishes

Sanctuary

architects are the most convicted poets

their diagram becomes our practicum
they retrieve the heart its minarets & pinnacles
to sanctify the bodies' residence
in hypostyle & gable, mibran & muqarna–

on heights to free belief from any need
like the pistil-centered rays through the rose-window
transform the sun into something more than light
& the soaring angles at the sightlines of the ziggarut
suggest a perpetual departure--air-without-end

& spirit's in the arch, the hard vissour,
rewarding calculations & finding
cool spaces for the soul that breathes beneath

from plane to plane, stone to stone, flute to flute,
building gardens in the fire of god's vacuity
& feeling the cornerstones sponsor stories of desire.

so enter what you are: the horizon unseen by anyone.

the sun of my Perfection is glass
wherein from Seeing into Being pass.

place re-places skin; succor's bodied in a building
inviting emotion to motion, moving room to room
to know rapture as an enclosed & infinite transparency

breathe the ease: be safe within the ziyyada.
for you are on foundations even on the windy roof,
where a dancer poses against the clouds
& as she raises her arms into an arabesque
the sky behind her falls in love with shapes again.

Manhattan Ghazwa

Miss DeBelliss had skies in her eyes.
But I remained far from my nine-year old wishes.
I'd have run a dictator's triathlon to win her affection
and sold my sister into slavery just to pull back her blue curtains
and come to know a smoothness that could assure me (wondering 'is
it true'?) does Saturn have such glorious rings?

she led us in phonics and in phonetics, in posture and the Pledge,
she threaded my right finger with ribbons to remind me which hand
covers the heart when we talk absently to the flag; she even led us
to part the silence with occasional Italian songs stolen from a second
floor Roman— *volare, volare, cantare.* She handed out maps and names
for us to study: was it a fisherman's state, or a shape in cattle-herding
country? What was that state's favorite fruit? Did you sniff those
mimeographs like I did to catch the glue and the hint of her perfume
and also to ask, did your parents approve that permission slip?
Can we (one day) permit all participation? Will you sign here, allow
your son or daughter to take tomorrow's field trip, down, to the top
of the World Trade Center?

Permission granted, I got permissive with dreaming.
I could smell her even from the back of the yellow bus
as we passed a fruit market's wood, shattered boxes, Bronx River slicks
and I re-dreamed her as a Scottish queen & me a liege to her golden rings
imagining battles on her behalf as we passed a rage of hollow buildings
cindered like the structures of Berlin; or graffito of Puerto Rican nationals
further south, pentagon sidewalks that gray-carpet a border for parks,
driving a center lane through the looming grids of scattered buildings

till our driver told us this is officially now Manhattan, kiddies:
there are no millionaires in the Bronx and no liege for queens
and no cathedral to speed by on your left, no jewel shops to comet
to your right and no narrow infinity of traffic lights converging
to blacktop and steel-heights, where one by one, we entered
elevators of desperate compression.

the huge cement swath on the south tower's roof was no footprint
from a remake of King Kong: I thought *Lord, please, give me a blonde in the*
center of any black hand, and give up to me what we couldn't call *sky*
because *look!,* I shouted, *we can't see the sky because we are in it*
and a penny dropped from this high would land like the weight
of an anvil on any walker far below; yet a flower blown off with a wish
would drift far over the river and become the train and gown
of five wives toward your future paradise

> *going up by burrowing down*
> *skyscrapers rise to nothing*
> *& no story's sweet beginning*
> *can conceive a happy ending*

Miss DeBelliss moved to Texas when I was twelve
and married a plebian; I grew up writing fables on dice
and allegories of ships anchored by dungeons of fish
& I drew her in every image that I imaged: pearl-rung,
safely castled, forever regal.

I even fashioned her a bracelet made of Saturn's moons

And I recalled her in the fall after the *ghazwa*
riding the ferry out to love across the harbor,
the nun next to me weeping at the burning
rubble, huddled about her beads & praying
as if she were trying to comfort the saints.

I pictured Rumi-become-Aquinas, asking
who will go up to the mountain of the Lord?
who will breathe God in the breath of flowers
that opens every night across the sky as peace
keeps its vigil to kindle the emptiness?
now, let the morning air bring the presence that angels
in amazement will watch. Love is that river; drink from it.
Love allures us within the green wheat.

I think she'd be proud of my psalms; maybe she wondered
had I grown up to be one in the stairs when the earth dropped
its burden to hell? & did she catch the fires live?
or was she sipping soy latte on a Dallas freeway, singing
to her own Faith Hill song, while on this end of the earth I wished
she'd never left, silver roars came streaming over our city,
serenading the garish sun.

The Address

Born at odds with the actual,
I'm a sworn enemy of the real.

May breezes inspire delusion
& lay a *mise-en-scène* on me.
I approach our uptown flat.
I recognize its round corners.
I jiggle the key as I remember,
just-so. The shocked tenant
learning we live there (again-now)
leaves. I'm engaged to a second
chance in the abandoned space,
left countless revolutions behind.

Trusting in a recuperation of routine
I know you're on your way home from work,
so I wait, clutching straws & sit. I'll grow older
by silence. But I won't jinx joy by weighing down
a flight of actual fiction with the leaden truth of false fact.
I won't embarrass us by shouting your name to the street
or put a hex on the address by shooing jittery sparrows that
sing & crowd the sill. I won't relent the courage to live
for reclamation. I won't grow up, don't bother, I won't *get
over it*. And I won't let words become reality-prose.
As soon as the door creaks its promise from the lobby, in time
to the tapping of your approaching footsteps, a partner in
this new life will shake me back to her other-here and not
even the soft gods will be sorry when I wake and learn
you never arrived.

An Alphabet of Elsewhere

here's deluded-clarity,
& an open birth-space for new letters—
vowels to caress the surface-work of consonants
& outline the daisy beds, mark a single *centafolia* rose;
help its petals stain a crazy path where she walks
& wonders & by wondering, writes:

can these fictions render this
mystery-slant of late morning
light? or the astonishment
of the encroaching after-rain sun,
squared-on-skin? how do you
articulate (with 'I's) such white bolts
of sun on the fire & fine stretches of black silk?
& how can you map, like a Dutch cartographer
the lining & the sweetness of the in-patterns?
can you know the coasts simply by pre-supposing an in-firing
& then proposing a furnace for the sea?
or let planets 'drown' in whatever waves the moon makes?
the image will do whatever you make of words
the blue shaken pane
the gyration of east wind
& God alive in the nape of Garbo's neck
risking the ludicrous
& saturating the precious with early-period blues
& rippling those blues with pink melancholia—a gospel of *alla prima*
like the long October sky that haunts us
after we've said good-bye to yet another lover:

and so what? so, the gods leave us like family
to make us free, free to conjure
modish faeries in homemade minis,
in velvet & in water-diamond-on-tights
transcription of a bitterness gone ambrosial

& phrases that extend being out beyond the plausible
in bodied-words time is a drawn-out terrifying nuance
& 'reading' is read as 'living'
language is a leaving, a selfish truancy,
syllabic chaos in the spirit of Sye-Ling Yun,
stroking characters on melon-colored books
& studying geese tracks along a sky
or on a moonless walk during war
recalling some past adultery
for its sneak-peaks & childish pleasure
like cinnabar cliffs & night-swimming
or blue shorebirds of Serpentine Island
& fishing trips with a young emperor,
out to the mouth of undiscovered seas

this is to come alive by writing
like Keats, young, imperial, yellow

half in love with easeful death

replacing craft with character-as-palace:
as existence-in-the-lines emerges ahead of meaning—

wise agnostic obsessions
& verse singing credos
far beyond the glottal stops—

waywardness is an unleashed perfecting impulse

enslaved in a sensorium, obey the only mandate, truancy—

the 'one' you are is a fiction
of the one you'd tried to read—

life is an alphabet of elsewhere,
a falling for declensions
where those better selves begin.

Circuit City

I'm part of a quick waiting line in Circuit City.
A doe-eyed register-girl asks me for my Visa.
Words are the only installment plan the heavens
left me. I should cut my losses with the lethal truth:
girl, my best friend was cremated today in Queens,
that spot on his back was a trick the angels traced:
in zero-air, the pale trembles of tree-fallen snow
gave back what the chapel fires made of him.
Loitering, waist-wrapped in winter wind,
I faced a long third down without a back.
He's air now. I left the other mourners to wish
my buddy back. I'm buying hardware
to amplify a hollow. I can revel in the speakers'
ambisonic sound, refuse elegies, and spin
Hendrix at Winterland, The Who in Leeds.
I'll windmill pain away, drop a Gibson on
the hippie-bed, pour whiskey on a bleeding palm,
and make like wise Montaigne: stop wondering
about the *why*, and feel the deep self-going
drop of it: write no-closure on oblivion:
it was a whisper, listen, it was a scream:
because it was him, because it was me.

Fellow Tenants & I Dream of Man Ray's
Nancy Cunard

nothing like getting drunk on nothing, or seeing merely for the sake
of wanting to see– bleeding oil paints, underneath the hushed breeze
of a fish-kitchen's ceiling fan, hearing its subdued purr & the jangle
& hustle of unseen walkers, busy cookers, fellow-feelers (I will think
of) as neighbors– out of respect for their mornings, I imagine the cat-
claw fights & the nasty family gatherings they'd lived out under
their own eyelids, last night, while our moon sat on Yonkers,
ignoring the toy-like, red-eye flights passing slowly in the dark sky
conveying sleepers to Montreal, Santa Fe, Miami: flyers, restless leg
syndromes, drowsy sitters & those hot meals that the blue-hosed
stewardess distributes– a poet dropping by for a beer reminds me
elements merge in the night, ships make tacks in the dreams– for one night
let's agree to dream the same dream, no narratives, no twisted
familiars, just a visage an artist made to excuse us from the burden
of making visions by ourselves: she's electric-awake, porcelain-white
she floats over sepia gloom & half-sleep –her profile is the pause of a
sugar band's bop– her eyes are jewel fires extinguished by the
intensity of their own lights, still in motion, she stares & her gaze is
precisely all we dream – her *lumen* is Pascal's image of the mind's
returning circuit (will we share such impressions while dog-walking,
coffee-schlepping, the next morning?) – will we agree she's the
image of us? I believe we can accept whatever is, is reflection & that
we, like she, can be captivated in a permanent fleeing where we are
settled by the self in a beautiful other.

In Praise of Our Lady of the Flowers

in answer to the philosopher,
dress the self in better questions
& breathe your purified anger

why Socrates? why query love
why when fish, shoe & flesh,
white-lilies & anus are enough?

why pedantry instead of extasy?
why history when I've stories
which spring from my eyes?

for I filched that tiny diamond
a gypsy-fish hatched; I tricked
the unguarded mercury-pool—

emote, for art is a criminal intention,
not merely an act but always illicit

the way poetry is a Saturday
when the lady of the house,
to clean, puts the mansion's
red velvet chairs & mirrors
& mahogany table into the nearby meadow
& the nymphs chuckle as a yellow finch
perches on her master-seat & mocks the passing cat—

that dying bitch, clawing through the lawn
faced with the feathered queen, seeks the bliss
of birdsong-ridicule — cruelty restores vitality
in its wounding, lust makes us delirious outcasts —
angels expelled from accepted heavens
rewarded by a perpetual tumble--

this is the falling
to impending extinction,
falling further, falling faster,
inebriated by the rush of air

bracing for a bang that never comes

Separation Agreement

fold up ten years,
five months
& four weeks
& I disbelieve age
or time could suddenly
become this final
near half midnight
clearing plates, washing silver
after a last meal together,
trying to reach past all ending
for the vague permanence
under fig branches where
the moon's light intrudes
speaking in cool darkness
crying *years*, you hardly
believe–as I do–our love
as if 'we' were but a day
that's ended.

Query

did you rent that
pink apartment?

the place you described
on our parting drive?

or are you blanched,
in blank exile, waiting,

wondering whether to
call me for the colors?

Yellow Fish

label the yellows: yellowfin, banana, morning sun, butter.
fish fritters, a glass of French ale on a windowsill.
sea-breezes change, sending cool, settled winds.
painters dab. violently, with love.
so she says, be generously abstract.
abstract is carnal.
representing is retreat. *c'est vrai*?
lemonyellow background, evenly canvassed, *oui*.
feels the heat of yellow in his hands, stroking the color brush
across: unsteady.
God is yellow and unsteady too. Aurora. Canticles.
she said color measures your own ability to live within what is.
Debussy strings yellow. Hear?
love is art. what Shakespeare sonnets: painting
in fresh numbers. so with seeing:
and then: your world goes yellow as the mood settles on you, opens
you out to a tone you have never lived with: ghastly in size, soothingly
deep, so soon your hand is soaring across the canvas in new time:
stroking gentle lapses of buttery yellow in wet lines: the flat definitions
of fish, and more: water, speed, aquatic swirls: and living all the while,
yourself in motion, pressing out shapes of worlds, dabbing and
drizzling morning sun for more: there: a new patch
of liquid sun about the fish.

La Conquête

remember the bad-ass cat of the *Maîtresse*
who walked the rail in the windstorm
& sniffing the pâté, devoured salmon?
We watched the stupid tom get soaked.
We honored a similar hunger as he ate.
Lock-limbed, mute, we conjured words
to redact the pain. We writ souvenirs:
ferocious minutiae-as-biblical emblems.

After the rain, a teaspoon you held over
your lips caught July & hid the tuck
& dimple of your grin. In *velo* under leaf-
shadow by the Bois, we broke to fruit
halves. Your face bloomed with freckles.
We ended the day in fury under the Pont-
Neuf, snipping fishing nets to free
the catch & reclaim the city for the Celts.

Children of the Islands

a burst of

electric confetti

    & a hesitation

of tendrils;

    pregnant lines

converge
    & capsize;

chords
    turn to music

in the quiet
    of the colors

& each thumb-clasp
    shapes

a mountain's
    tip;

& is that trout
    that spills from

a whirling parade?
    or petal-fangs

that ring out & run
        from what they are

morphing into
        the wave, scallop & give

of what they will become?

Sufi Bricolage of Birds

many is one
in a multifarious
union

that makes multiples
of what the erotic glance
of god returns as infinite

& makes a poem sing of
a planet-spread fantail
of stars

a first movement names
the pelican a sea-coward
a second fugue
disses the frail finch
& one quatrain
pegs the blue-necked parrot
as echoing Narcissus

the yapping bird is a metaphor
for existence: only the hoopoe
knows to ask who's the vocalist
nagging, trilling a mimicry of course
& crystal spring-in-rock cleft trickle?

who sings with wings open & ignores the lesson of Daedalus?
who knows where Sama's never heard? who's seen the salmon-
colored savior route a flock to gods by singing beyond the tired
after-self: who solves the loveknot with an aria beyond desiring?

we wait for Sheba's signal-fire
trusting the blaze of honey-
hair on black, we pray
against a leaden dark
to grace the desert night
& sway the killers cease.

Poissenneux

Tables make long beds for copper-sheen sole, each smacked down, flaps over onto two & two to a third till they are five-or–eleven–schools–crowded abundance, miracles & twin yellow eyes rung round in ink-black, staring into a nothing that is–the town's collage, the sea-idyll, the frenetic spikes of sound, then the murmuring, the money-rings & the inquiries, the rational bounds of the market square–ruined soles under a hail of ice shards are washed clean, blood-red rivulets match the petals of potted tulips & swards of green leaf make a tiffany-like glass-run—such an intricate staging for such a messy harvest—the apron-cutters at their reveries, the elderly watchers under the mistral, the symmetries of fin-tip, the topsail of silk, the Breton sky, the ocean-toned, icy hue, and its variations are arpeggios for the eyes—shimmer of brine on rain-soaked, bay-plump & silver-finned blues.

Evangel

Imagine an apostle baked under Thessalonican morning sun. Jesus Christ has been dead a long time. He's unreturned. But this saint's heart, tided by fire-tongued grace, breaks over border-walls of a dumb, dry land. Here coitus is king, and queen, and in the fresco's moment, he's found his rest sitting on the marble ledge in the unconverted art of Apollo's temple. His rose-pink robe is wrapped snugly round his long limbs. You'd think his portrait painter was born palming the counterpoints of God's geometries. Still, there's a resurrection emerging from a blue scroll he holds. But the apostle is exhausted beyond his purpose. His future-wary eyes are already closing off on the blood-rush of life within. Fading like hope-letters scribbled from prison, cautioning each heathen in answer to a sickening ritual: My brothers! Do not suddenly lose your heads or alarm yourselves at some oracular utterance! His fixation is its own proof: belief is to be lost in this drawn, forgiving face, set on the very kingdom he was born to teach.

Study of St Peter, After Masaccio

1

His copper gold halo circles over soft white halo circles
and so, to start, a penciled halo drawn in an easy turning
circle, smoothly perfect circle penciled easily back round
the circle. Halo. Softwhite hair layered in curls under his
halo, curvy locks drawn on a round scalp, drawn easy
enough with a loose grip, easing into a looser trembling
grip to let the curls overlap, drawn feathery, curls penciled
loose to an end with smokeshading for the start of his
neck. Perfect shade scratches. Softmakings.

2

How the blue mantle gives off a sea green shadow under
his bunchy sleeve, drawing the shadow in cloudy circles,
the charcoal pressed to paper first lightly then giving off
sharp lines, fast lines, smoky soft and fast, penciling down
his arm with light shaking traces smoothing straight to the
robe cuff, a tremble-gentle circle of cuff, tracing down
wrist-to-hand and round to closed fingers, fleshy knuckled
fingers, drawn soft. The fingers of the other hand peek
under the sleeve touching the orange gold, a tender hand-
peek under the robe folds. Perfect. Also-perfect down from
his left shoulder in fabric-light lines, traces with shadowed
folds, bends, how the robe glows orangegold: a fresco
orangegold: colourheat: heaven rich orange. And the sun
on his robe darkens the thick folds.

3

Down to draw feet, penciling a liquid outline, tracing feet,
toes, a shaded heel, rounded in half circles, almost perfect
now, back up, tracing again along the waves of fabric line
fronting his robe, trembling lines, penciled so, and perfect,
and how much perfect in the soft lines, the body full now
even without the finished face: Saint Peter: fisher of men:
deep eyes: solemn boned: staring down at his own hand
extended there, paying out as Jesus says to pay, handing
over and knowing in his moment, in the giving, from deep
dark Palestine eyes looking at his loss, tribute money: eyes
telling us all the while how much more than coins he
hands to the leaning man in red.

Delicious Trouble

after Dorothea Tanning's Birthday, 1942

first know the peach & slo-fade pink of her feet & then, say,
paradisial toes, her skin barely there on the dull grain of the
planks, a high-rise, low-rent loft floor, where she's a bodied
spirit & ethereal master, a kin to the daemon, the face-muse &
giggling-death, her pet, alight, already, present, near her, the
short-winged griffin's seduction by uncertainty, all that's
beautiful & bright waits, where a devil's dream and an angel's
nightmare twine to one image, where colours ask for your
own response, as if, through her open doors, you could speak
in tongues like the painter herself & turn, toward more, one
door of a lifespan opening perpetually out to the other, where
there's more than air, more than line, much more too than
meager 'fulfillment,' here's a self-portrait of possibilities,
come, see your self standing as this artist, stripped of closure
& grown richer by being what she shares.

her painting's a psalm & think on what Ernst said precision is
her mystery & I add, her images salve the stark convulsions of
love, see? the Dietrich-features of her face? bring only forms
Plotinus would recognize (*this is the spirit that Beauty must ever
induce, wonderment and a delicious trouble*), escorting the
horribly infinite into time, so springs an essence, an
incalculable series where she draws, she paints & she sculpts
through doors & levels of spirit she already lives by, honored
or not, painting is her own essential teaching: soon you'll read
the chemistry of that perfection, seen here, in her gown,
morphing into fever-green branches of Daphne, nipple-
branching, suggesting electricity inherent in her pale skin's
vibrancy, in the brambles, in the hawthorns, even in the urban
studio, fertile net-works—and all the American wild blooming
at her hips.

so blush before this patrician blonde, because you'll remain less beautiful than she is – unashamed, she flaunts her regalia, its purplegold jacket sleeves spilling lace frills, declaring her self emblematic of every artist, the blue bloods, the wicked species, aristocratic scion of creation, daughter of Aphrodite & Lucifer, a promise-breaker, atavist, colorist, imagist, classicist, opening (here, literally) her loft doors, unafraid, courting raw exposure, her bare breasts, rosepink, somehow her skin suggesting the Celt, tiny blooms of aureole, gradations of blush, the coy wrap of thumb around a gawdie belt, Shakespearean confidence, faith in the acrobatic risk of conflation, confusion, exhilaration—her disinterested eyes express welcome by farewell, at once, which (after all) are the seductive quantities of all elegance—farewell-as-welcome—set rapture to intricate music & kneel to know her trinity of vertigo, Venus, *volupté*.

Muse

The sun shoaled your freckly arms so insistently its light
on you nearly made a cuckold of me. You snored like
exhausted Cassandra. I dipped my pen into your roux-
pool & scribbled characters on the note-table. The first
work-note suggested *make an extended metaphor of the
morning glory*. But I had to run off the banal impulse to
imprison such a rhapsody in the bare cage of form. With
patience, gray morning gave me license. Overnight, the sea
acceded & let whitefish make the sky's face. At home, you
were up at your zinger-tea, reading my hopeless line-
notes. Your nightwear turned our kitchen into a stage-for-
hot-roses. Its patterns made a dawn constellation of the air.
You said you were embarrassed about my black query.
What more in the world would lovers like us need besides
the fantasia we've made of our unity? Why, when we have
such precision, would we need to make a morning glory
into a metaphor? And why denude a bride–green eyes and
all–as if she were some ordinary flower?

Lines for an Irish Dancer

for fleet
sweeping feet
spinning reels
fiddles for the air
word crazy epistles
of could-be's
& yesterdays,
still burning
glow-lit hearth
in our hearts
in our books-
in-progress,
vivid, sharp
like Mondrian's
Evolution (with stars
for her shoulders)
our records,
acoustic-electric
dark geometry
lit by colours
blooming
sexy-smart
we write each other
past bad weather,
calling our selves
out of ourselves,
shoplifting kisses
& candy-fishes
sealing treats with stickers
& a red screen's secrets
(in green & blue
see China right
in front of you)
even in Eire
in drizzle
on bridges

your umbrella poses
will be Orient-elegant
in oyster-tinged air
guitars by blue-
doors, soloing
we warm
our winter skin
in lyrics
circling round
& trying
(vacant
as laughter
in lonely summer)
finally forgetting
the artifice
of ties
for play
is the liberated
intelligence
of instinct
& life is hap-
hazard poetry
like *The Pillow Book*
like your Westside
goddess-grace
& black chic
show of tights
and synchronized
kicks & spins
all gestures
from the sources
dancing blood
& lithe-finesse (you
hear?) this music's
blasting beneath
our separate ceilings
not faraway,

coming close,
in your eyes,
the centrifugal song,
the dance of desires,
smiles, opening time
into surprises.

Bleeding Hemispheres

world & round
whirl crazier
& more of it you know:
the earth's air
is mauve;
her forefingers splay
reds on avenues adverse
to clarity and to color
Manichean palettes
& an Australian dock,
the black and white
emigrant port & the March
blizzard grilled on a black, East Village guardrail
& green escarpments painted grey;
there's a creepy achievement to all painting:
it subtles us a world crazier
and more of it than you know;
pray the marker
makes the inside circle of the ceilings blue;
arrive up slippery ladders
watch how time
checks out for instabilities
& a side-view of a crazed doctor's anatomy
falls to be tangible & proves
the cold veracity of the day-dream

Eireann Blues

escaping the withering heat-
wave through a reunion in the
cold *duomo* chocolate café
where we stare at our salads
& study what isn't; our blue
eyes dart round the glass,
stilled by reflective energies
like kids rapt by puddle-gazing
& strung out on sugar highs

I channel *fair mirrors on mazed hearts*
toward your red brow where the autumn dreams

but we can only wonder what to do
with punishing, humdrum silences
& tensions of a go-along, redundant ignorance
that rings us round Village streets & doubles back
on us, imprisoning us in every corner of our sleep,
far from what love knows we've tried to forget, apart,
awake, separately at a loss with others,
aware of the skin's wisdom waking years
on top of years & that question toward a world beyond our words—
does he, does she know our lives must be this love?
or am I spending a rare blue currency
on the delusion of an isolate dreaming?

The Red Fez

like orange clouds, or melon-colored fish-craft
capsized by the gale-force, we wake from the nightmare
of a simple life; a poem's *vers libre* begins
in memory's two-step, making fables of the misremembered
& ungodly epics of what was half-believed
& weaving sworn memoirs of that fairy-tale-desire;
once upon a time, you found your great grandfather's
red fez & ordered me to bring round the non-negotiable supplies;
a French easel, strapped on my back, was eye-candy for the 1-riders;
at your landing you waved me up, like a figure out of Georges de Feure
that languid river-flow woman, in search of the infinite
in your gossamer black slip, scarf & the red fez;
flounce, tough to paint but not so much its fickle
play of light: folds, in-folds and its letting-go;
you assured me the stockings were from Nice
& the blue divan, a family gift from Dutchess
& the setting sun over there (you know by now)
as Horus heading home to the kingdom of isn't;
the day watched us from the mirrored run of the Hudson;
rivers and streams and rivulets are arteries of the earth's
enduring passion for carving its own tracks--part green,
part dream-glass; all cities are built by water currents;
geomancy is an instinct of the skin;
the red of the fez was bold as hell, enriched by yellow dragons
that festoon the foreground & chase the scaled tails of gods,
so manic we named them for a dervish ritual;
whirligig insanity is just the nature of invention;
you resorted to writing *God isn't a Daddy,*
God made us only to please Himself
that's a blunt, brave faith Aquinas might accept,
the prime mover is a failed artist just like us,
just a subject, predicate & self-reflexive object
like Matisse & Bonnard, writing selfishly of the jeweled light
& Tahitian loins & maybe, in their next life,
studying the blue of this divan, nicknamed June;

you said your great grandfather was restless,
a typhoon wherever he wandered,
part Arab, gypsy, a copper-bearded genius
a mage to many courtesans
(I saw) as you stretched your left (stocking) leg
you teased your shoe-tip's amethyst
your pose corresponded so fluidly
to the inscrutable slides & figuring of the Indian ink,
watery, marigold-green, the river-light struck the transom–

red is a destiny-gift from the ancients to us
Egyptian, Russian & English sojourns
contained like scents in its fabric;
I mixed Hong with Akako, Japanese red,
'child of red' with Persian Gulrang,
American Maroon, Fluvus & Aurleus,
Brinley & Ross; a panoply of reds emerged
in blood-bright tints haloing your dark hair
like tribal chants that fill the humid air
& captivate the dusk; like red rain, before
a festival of torches & the red flames of unspoken,
under-earth urges, just like painting the unrepentant
glow of your white shoulders; you stared as you sat
across the loft: pupil-night-browns & planets
of incredible promise—a gaze, guiding my hand
assuring me with zodiac-precision, inspiration is
the unmasked face of lust; these brushstrokes of red
are the actual fez & the pay-out of what we'd
planned for, in silence, standing for years
closing in on astonishment, before sleep, all those summers,
each heartbeat of ours is now the mimesis of an art beyond us:
the model (effortlessly) is as much the painter as the master is;
the tale carries on after us: a song sung beyond our intentions
we are in verse: envoys of its fragile silence, its dreadful pulse.

Cascading

the train channels a swath through the saffron
fields of Bohemia churning toward Germany;

bands of sunlight burnish & copper your hands
as I press a white finger to your lips, to hush us

you touch my sex to flesh out your own —
there aren't words for the extremities of love

but cascading—a chattering world surrounds us
& wave-onto-wave, how it whispers its melodies

giddy, we swim, up & in—we rip into its tributes.

St. Brigid's Song

In a barren rotunda he's
the emperor of a kingdom
named Contre-Femme:
Il Duce bans bare knees
from St Peter's & he's
never been a match for
a pagan roundel written
after a woman's freckled arms:
his liturgy has it in for the pink
& he blanches at the nipple & the slip.
She defies his genuflect & comes,
singing-so, her trad-glamour's
always fresh—its shocks of pearl
roil damp air with an anarchy
of extasy & every thing turns
into some thing else—Dublin's blues
go saffron in eyes of a downtown mage
& all flags are rendered orange
within the red of her withering flames:
chords re-christen London skies
& Rasta-ballad lays the measures
proving jigs to be electric & the lullaby,
a dirge & every anthem, a whisper
dispelling a molester's con
& the crippling myths of the Garden Fall—
so play on, envoy, Francis Villon
is listening, sing from the isle of the smithy
as you play & shake the fig leaf free,
remind the lips the fruit is real

Blue in Green

over-order mounts
        a lack of jazz—
& that much control
        will kill a man—
let go & go, be
        & be sweet
dexterity
be as unexpected
as   tanned fingers
digging pulp
        & fingers
dexterous, lick the slick
        mangoslip—
hang the fruits
        of winter
from the rusted hooks of the sun
        till it rains
        juice
on the bare chests of everyone—
        skin-so-soaked
turns gold   & goes electric
as the crystal rush
        of hot rum that makes
hands   receptive as creeper-
vine tracing
        spider-fingered
pink flora & brushing
        off a blonde's
summer-soft perm,
        darting quickly
as the christomarie flies
        to carry such changes,

far & riff & follow
       the stickle-back
is to be   motion
       & a soothing cruise
into her green eyes'
       coronae of radiant blues

Fishing for Amber

along the wandering
midcourse come answers
the apple basket answers
the orange dress answers
her sidelong smirk
& young diamond answer
the question is what am I to see?

thrown back on joy & streams
coursing beneath the skin
dissolving that occlusion
hell, a medieval fiction—
evict the neutered cynics
disavow the porn of piety
& the pious college scribes
versifying hair shirts
about cancer & crows
feeding their past,
courting Thanatos

free disorder
the odd is clarion
let in the terrifying answers
let the orange dress answer
let her truant giggles answer
let the French painter
wash you in blues

by the magic of the she-devil
who renews her taste for life
thanks to the wooing of the sweeper

the country's twisted trees
yielding unreal cherry,
yielding these angel-nuts
& feeding a stream-bed,
stream & springs of mottled light
source of freckles
you follow the flow like gospel
& are freed, loose & lost
in a fisherman's valley
closing in on bliss
up on the amber ridge
passing the burgundy slip
being covetous
of raw possibilities
rapt by white feathers
tracing the infinite along lips
half-sleeping, dreaming the teacher
into Daphne, under the song
you expect, open as rose,
rising, wide as sunflower
loosening pedestrian restraint
disrobing in the sun
stripped lighter than need
levitating on a subtle rush
a disoriented homecoming
you are arriving to a vision of your self
you'd seeded so precisely
in the manacled years,
under the sad regime
here you are the poem
rewarded by colour
on the amber ridge
the echo of a bacchanal
& promise of the real god–

the young lovers are in hiding
they are somewhere else
much farther than the night.

Bouquet

I remember well even when all I recall
reveals its spaces in reverse—six years since
I last saw you–I see begonia brightening
& stirring your smiles—this close-distance
of fiction's memories is dumbfounding,
eclipsing the wide April sky that isn't
yet wakes me incredulous about sense
so sparsely somehow flourishing & by desire
the lost passion outgrows itself–colored like
the purple heliotrope that snakes about the
darker stems & struggles to be seen
in the orange bouquet you hold.

Ars Poetica: No more politics with no more boys

in this exile, breathing days
we do our best to make our-
selves at home in the belly
of a creature not of our design.
we crouch low, as if the marble
ground might help us rise, brace
for the Penn Station walker
with a suicide strap after eternal American
Fridays as we walk into the infernal dream
of another God (only he knows). do as the sign
says: if you see something, say something

an angry teen, not cut out for action, I used to cut
Natural Science to read family-hell with Franz Kafka's
Gregor Samsa in the Catholic library; a reading that inspired me
to mail *vita nuova*-style epistles from the Farley GPO,
to Salt Lake City & Santa Cruz & a former holiday nest in Puerto Plata.
today I do my part for the sacraments of seeing:
I note the blue head of the green
African parrot, perched at the end of a staff
which a man in the Panama hat takes into
Baby Watson Cheesecake one autumn Tuesday—

when it comes to teaching 'rigorous' thinking
& protestant exegeses, no one stares down Beauty
& whips her so for her allurements like I do;
when my Brazilian co-sponsor, Bettina, made a butterfly wink at me,
just above her belt line, I chastised her for a disturbing lack of decorum
(& cranky Horace backed me up)—sex & murder, the Roman decreed
(like bowel movements) must happen offstage, so as never to offend
the humanity of those who've lived too weakly

so locate the sublime in daily news of global accident, dateline
unknown, like when an Ecuadorian junta starts a nuclear war
& I ask Bettina what the fuck were her español Fuhrers thinking?
she says she doesn't read the papers but guesses 'radiation' is vicious,
from the mere syllabic star-punctured sound of the word itself.

outside, the world is the purest form of rage
quicksong angels are unemployed
poetry's a calm inside made of ribbon-tied chaos.
Bettina clacks her tongue & recites Lorca on leaving the day
with his possible concretions of impossible minutes
during a seminar-break an unhappy Lothario told me
he'd needed Bettina more than his own tongue
& he adored her eyes beyond the call of the Virgin
he'd tried to win her with Corona & dance
but she was too elliptical in her arguments
she'd picked apart the false premise of gooey sonnets
as if she were born measuring end-rhymes & dithyrambs—
(one final sidebar, if I may: why don't no one seem bothered
about the lethal winter that will soon blow in from Nicaragua?)

Go back to sleep, senators, if you haven't already, sleep
peacefully on the courthouse steps of them judges who've had their way
with our privates: what we do behind the curtain does not, these days,
decide presidents: look, you wanna send a message, try Western Union,
you wanna write a 'real poem', go dig up your ratty Norton
I'm here to pass this hello off as a disguised good-bye
Nueva York is all I wanted: the empty lot & old lights
along the Harlem River, take me home most directly
by passing under a precipice
I re-live the strain of immigrants
I've lived here nine hundred and seventy eight lives
Ireland ain't just a pock-marked cow pasture to me
the train-calm bubbles up the water surface
& even my sneakers are soothing:

the minutes lessen into names of stations
the goat song in Lothario's account of his rejection haunts me:
he told me he'd told her he'd give up sex
until the day of the altar came
but his Bettina-Beatrice said no such wedding would ever come
& she called him a jackass as she spun on her heels
claiming she don't want to talk no more politics with no more boys
& then she walked out of this form of life & vanished
into the choke hold of some mofo-Don Juan,
a charming punk from Rikers who *The New York Times* said
she'd never told a soul was waiting, committed to wed her all along.

Milan Romance

it's a goddess' kinetic elegance:
how her hands, in a reflex-dance,
conceal her quick self-satisfied
giggle fit:

once composed, she's attentive
grace: shy & sure, like the subdued force
of her velvet basque & its wild, slick-
black knot of bow:

she's a flautist
in flight from Michigan,
in the creamy stanzas of Milan,
making her mind the heart's bible
& burning for the hall's
orange & baroque poses:

its yellow-painted flora is
fresco-sensuous,
like the almost-papal,
gilt-lily mirror she kisses:

like light, her lip's secret
flutesong,
making delicious moan
upon the midnight hours,

shivering the mirror in soft timbres.

So Full of Shapes is Fancy

come to wonder like the rose grower
wake your skin to the late promises
of light: watch dusk color the white
garden wall: be a pink-tinted canvas
for the courtyard: her leaf-droopy greens
& young budded flowers:
cowslip, geranium & chamomile,
thick clustered stalks, palmetto,
creeper vines & wet palms,
a trimmed yellow rosebush
& a *coco de mer*; twilit air
holds the scents of needs
drenched & stretched, eased
into an afterglow: even the feast lingers,
luscious: grilled peppers, sushi
zucchini & seared tuna

the Roman blonde, Linda, is a cosmetologist
& coiffeuse (& actually) English:
her paisley day-dress is discarded: purple-
pink silk by an empty planter;
as Linda in white fire
goes about the business of love:

she's tracing painted canopies,
painting ruby-tips & writing recipes
for gems: courting the mild dove:
seeking abundance:
in the tiny & enticing late light
into amazing arrangements:
plucking flowers & fingering
rich strings, crafting all-about
spring gifts into her own
wave-layered & rose-petal choker

The Transit of Venus

Like an artist stepping from an unfinished canvas
you leave our loft & head out discreetly for Mass
tiptoeing, like a figure out from *The Eve of St. Agnes.*

You brush your hair & I hear the whush
of blonde wisps. I catch the clack of your sling-backs
that lay bare the percussive sin leaving itself.

I'm spiritualized by fires that won't go out. I sleep
& dream of orange light, mudflats near Perth
& the heft of yellow on cliffs and rock-cut,
a Pacific canyon airing blue space to Manly
& Sydney's Gap, grasping, for what's the word,
or the song, or the tag for the goddess
of bay-winds that carry the caws of species
I've never seen or wings in horizons
that remind me I exist at the discretion
of an ecology more intricate than any math we can ever know?

Lives pass. Hours quicken. The door opens, your jangling
& refinement take me back, back to the body & blood.
My waking breaks with your kiss.
You're back with tea & enlivening irony
We play ping-pong with a ball of back-dated words:
'mischief' 'codpiece' & 'treat' & 'telephone dispatch'.
Your roommate needs down-time to recover her New York ennui.
So we have space to stage newer plays
& cook exotica to our hearts content
& sketch the stems growing from the wattle
in your day-dress, straps slender as you are,
ethereal as the elegant trouble that swims through
the grays of the green in your eyes.

You say all the stage is a world & turn round & step out of spilled fabric. The sooty window above the slop-sink projects a clarion tease of light. *Sui generis,* fingertip-precise our benediction begins. Our birthrights align. Our skin pays arbitrage to the nerves & by dispersing exchanges our differences for the profanity of a delicate sameness.

Psalms after a Tempest of Stars

if waking God would be his death

who was it authored the dictatorship
of divinity set apart from human skin?

and was it strung-out prophets
who made God a blank messiah
staring back from virgin frescoes,
ebonied on prayer beads & trucked
out for their sentimental crucifix?

who said earth needs human minds to know it?

who verses sonnets in imitation of
a bleeding greengage and the natural hangars
of kinglets? who transcribes the ventriloquism
of sparrows, dive-bombing the orchard (*facile à
confondre avec l'encre* Waterman) veering
into patterns of flying fish, floating seahorse
& concentric elisions in ink-washed flights?

who rhymes cool shadows with hot sands,
or builds sounding vessels from broken nouns?

who strikes propositions into songs

& who will find the verbs to give them wing?

Goldfish

feeling's awe-full, each instant's
a surfeit: to truly be means
moving unconfined in frames—
lovers know love's a deluded effort
to square a roundel that eludes them
at its very naming: life's liquid as this
confluence of goldfish that breaks in
auburn & russet, explodes in ocher,
burnishes red pixies, brown shards,
curls the sea-greens & imperial plaque
swimming loosed by cyclical blues
& bubbling air in its viscous tempura
that will never sustain containment:
already beyond her self, the ivory muse
stares back at us, aware 'love' is
a silly fiction—a hybrid-fetish
phrase of cowards & scholars:
her grin knows how the future's
No overwhelms the present-Yes
& displaces reason & confuses
what you hoped you'd be
with what you merely are
facing a colored miasma in motion,
immersing the self in going
& making a mockery of the body's force.

Harbour Song

delicious levity
is the credo,
climbing a bluff–
windswept-russet
& salt-breezes —
synaesthesia
as the evening's
flower settles
among wind-birds —
ruff & reeve,
cutters & strong-
winged whimorets —
as we are,
so we write —
love means turning life
to riotous color
worshipping
an elusive kiss
as voices drift
from the wharf & turn
the air to counter-point —
barrel-chested Dominican fishers
emptying afternoon nets,
shouting their Spanish obscenities —
laughter of underpaid slaves,
mingling & making harmony
with the flapping & slapping
of grouper & flounder,
fruit de mer, farmed for a deity —
the Irish-American day-queen —
raison d'etre for the sloops
& for the brawn
& for the strenuous haul
for the stained dock
& exhausted fishers —

the elusive shades of her fair skin
mimicking the bay's respiring —
its crest & ebb
& surf-crash,
cresting
yet again,
as slow, out-going foam —
cascando -- thin-fitness —
the ocean's essence
is fluid openness —
an amoral bliss
forcing philosophers
to sing accompaniment
to a dangerous & stray
fickle wonderment of syntax —
a lingua franca
a raw *noesis*,
free of puritans' addiction to 'truth' —
flaunting even ludicrous 'rejected' titles —
Contralto of May, Lace-Flag of the Sands;
trusting the orange lust of the sun,
drawing faith from meshed scents
singing original responsorial psalms
in the sacraments of fun – freckles,
a fedora & out-of-place gloves —
this is the Easter-tide bounty —
its white-capped greens
& regal blues,
bluest in the deeps
where red & yellow starfish
warm the coral
& guppies burst in watery golds, swarming over the cress.

Cressida: An Isle Quartet:

palm

joy starts in the cool sunless corner and it lingers over the body because the light's imperial privilege is all this remaining landscape: a square well cupped by a blue-tin protector, then the sandy fore-yard where a palmetto bed thrives, robust greens compete against each before the bed itself is lost to the rest of the view—the orange grove, trumped by the royal blue sky itself—its blue is bottomed out by rolling nimbus—here the imbalance of vision is measured by the clouds & then comes back to the cool sunless corner where Cressida stands in a light-slashed palm shadow—she's a luxury ranch-hand herself—in white jeans, comet-boots, brown leather vest, a tan earned far from umbra, her sun-kiss won from a beach and sunny cove on the other side of earth—but here, she stands to become the intersection of arrival & rest: go on, her eyes encourage yours, vanish into the fore-yard, run the yard's sun-bleached steps & have the courage to lose yourself sooner than you'd like, in an ether of ever-after, given instinct, her eyes suggest, I'll follow your going: we'll make haste slowly, pass by laborers busy butchering the mangrove trees, razed for the regime of the glare's unforgiving blaze.

sunstone

this grove, likely sacred for long-dead purposes we'll never know, no matter how long busy diggers excavate what isn't there—Cressida's content with the abandoned stone, jutted ledge & sooty dirt ambience of ruin, here in a pocket just beyond the beach—a moss & weather-wracked temple—so in love with present intensities she's uncurious about the unfathomable past & respectfully sits at the off-center of her own image—barefoot, at peace among the remains of some god's portico, the sides of her feet dusted by attractive particles—gray, brown & crystal sands—a glittering slipper the spirit let go, like the temple's ghost trees & its faithful who are lost to shambles of belief, left without a capital of martyrs—these believers absconded the isle before the armada of language-makers arrived & choked the harbour & stabbed the virgin dunes with their colorful cloth-bearing spears, striking stakes on behalf of the rulers: all those know-better thinkers worlds away from what they claim.

blanche

if white's the absence of colour then what presence
conflates itself with the dragon-fish outburst & imploding
rainbow-after-nature? these ruptured flagons spill yellows,
orange & blues which roil in the once-white seat where
Cressida plays out her copper-toned dishabille, clad only
in a white balloon blouse, bordered by floral panels, the
dark yellow rays that give rise to pale petals: as the white
does for the pink, so it does for the blue & even the ivory
warp & weave of the wicker seatback suggests white is the
precise answer to the question so few ask: what colour is
that light-borne skein of absence, that absence that's
neither calm nor busy, neither muted nor sheer, yet is so
perfectly neutral it can hardly be described as no-thing?

flosculus

leave the politics of silk outdoors to die like a salt-coated slug in a patch of sun by the crazy path & come inside the glass room of the thatched villa, here to feel how much silk reveals by its concealing—check out Cressida's play-hood, which is a black hand-me-down throw from some former princess: see how the silk marks the circumference of her coffee-coloured pupils, see how it spells out a welcome-bow above fern-like rushes that seem to be forever taking shape over her black screen: a flesh-colored silk finger guides its own inside out: sweet *flosculus* pressed to let the seer (her self) in on that recess which gives more rewards for each touch, then the black paints the legs in those sun-shot glitter unparalleled in the named universe, unspeakable for what they do to the nerves, those cells, reserved for logical functions, get to know how subtly subtraction quickens the heart & makes way for the paradox of an addition that takes precisely all it's given.

Invisible Sydney

groundless,
over-domed by sky
& wealth & youth itself—
it's all glare
all horizon,
as broken bay
& opera-house
of sun
refracting fish-fin
across the sole harbour
any ship could enter
& into the familiar
strangeness
of a shaded yard
hybrids
of tiny bird-
flitting blooms,
blue eyed grass
setting borders
across purple
kinesthetic designs,
box-white checks
that band about
an evening's black selections
& end with the body's favorite tip
& touch cells that know
no end to honey
indicating the very-more
that is almost there
by placing her ivory
finger in the hollow
that lives in the space
of the stamen.

Thaw

A St. Patrick's Day storm by evening
turns the scrub-yard into grounds
of fluid change: a thaw that's nothing
less, or more, than living-death.
& I'm the waters, much as
I'm the 'earth' I named, to place
it apart, as if this planet
were a place beyond my being.
But why not stop the con
call the world by my own
surname & beware what
becomes me once I'm gone?
One day, a body, another,
ash, atomized into an atmosphere
too fine to have kept me in the first place.
Then is now, in that now is
the moment's unbecoming.
Loss is what's most worth living,
for living, essentially, alienates.
Holding-on results in a series
of incredible losses: like the pale blues
which the diamond surrenders
into silver, like the winter below
my window which thrives so visibly
at the start of its own dissolving.

Queen of the Aire

I bet the literal fool you went and married
never encouraged the odd and never invited
you to unmask your self in a new disguise.
I bet he never suggested you try black-trim
boots and that Miss May mink hat which, in
wearing, inspired you to pen yourself *Queen
of the Aire.* I guess that lawfully wedded sport
never peeled off the dense sheath, pair by pair,
exposing *l'espoir* & each god's different gifts.
And I sense your realist knows no words beyond
some stale reachable diction. How ignorant is he
of seapeach and dockwhite? And of the conchpink
clematis sprig & small-flowered soaproots?
Does he know the body's skin is a metaphor
for the more-in-less? And will he be a witness
when a painter kneels forward to face the futility
of Logos and savors the bounty of your palette?

Carp

carp is Chinese for advantage,
I remind myself, loving my life,
at the empty shore, reeling, my
carp swinging wildly alive
in wave-catching light, lake
fin-fished water sprays my face
laughing,
I leave,
carrying my carp
to Lan Ling's house on the hill:

her peach tree, young swallows
& almond blossoms:
where the gone-dusk stinks of lilies:

she wakes
as a song breaks on clouds
& stirs, washes;
barefoot: we celebrate
my night's catch
the moon-gleam warming
my finger-lemon
finds her lips & opens
her profile in light,
white as kingfisher's
wings
whispering yes

Nativity

There's a rumor someone slashed
the super's fat throat & tonight
we're stranded by unexpected wind
gusts. Black night breathes & low,
heavy, bomb-dropping December
rings in its own chills.

My sloe-eyed, small-boned,
whiskey voiced neighbor (aptly
named Jackie-O) nails a red
holiday wreath onto her door,
forbidding anyone but herself
to enter her passage in the season of light.

Odette's *Cattleyas*

I am dating online. I pass
on a Queens CPA. Certain I'll
never meet a second Cinderella,
I re-read Proust's mythic memoir,
studying a social masquerade
& pledge-pin betrayals in French.

I am redeemed by Odette's *cattleyas*:
flowers of fiction more tangible
than clothing: natural, satin-like,
they resemble organic fabrication
and their feigned garden artifice
helps Swann feel them as if real,
the way vowels and consonants
lift real-folk blues of boredom behind
speech & how the Long Island Sound
reveals the tide-surge by harboring
us from it.

Just as yesterday, decades ago,
I knew her skin was luminous
through her blue stockings' veil
and I thought her static sadness
indicative of a lifting mystery.

The glass slipper barely fit.

I took a vow to *partage*. I married
estrangement. The cumulus clouds
gave no sign of the sun's glaring hints—
and its absent-presence proves I lived
by holding what she never showed.

The New York Collection

Come, morning, come hard-hatted
fashionistas to pin silver leggings
into an island's granite & come map
fifty-eight floors of sequin and raise a towering gown.

Wake up where the morning ground robes sycamores
in mottled tan & damp, leafed accessories, measure,
cut & stitch a warehouse worth of hot green
onto gray shapeless acres, stitch yellow
to the river's blue & silver boa
& seam azure to the afternoon.

Follow the evening, with its dusky
thigh-robe, sleeves swirling in pink
nimbus, follow windy chiffon with dolphins
at the breakers, besting the clownfish
that leap in orange at the cuffs.

At the shore, netted magicians
draw bracelets from the river,
stones painted in Oaxacan palettes
& roped by Chinese string, making wrists
something more than merely American:
foreign-born-glamour & native-driven-kinks,
like an earth-toned treacle dress for a mountain terrace.

Later a trapeze top & black flounce skirt that surrenders
to the moon & whitens night under your black gauze.
By midnight, it's vamped into a city-ensemble
to unveil in the plush-red comfort of the opera box.

The next-day it's a memory-vest
& the outback hat for a Losaida brunch
& torn Levis with tattered windows
revealing garden-bossed hose, white
as gods, white as communion
weaves tinged to off-yellow,
white to remind autumn its
lingerie was always summer.

To fashion time
& laugh like this
is to clear the toxic debris
piled by imploded hopes
& live out a lust dressed by love
where the fall never
takes a choke hold
to the long day, here,
among seers, artists & doers,
dreams walk in broad daylight
& we are the stanzas, the racks of accents
& we are spring metaphors that magnify a miracle of bodies.

Masque

more than anything 'authentic'
would suggest, your disguise
reveals more spirit than anything
you've worn before

too savvy to be Snow White, you'd
never cut it as wizard or witch
& you're too much the ghetto-born snob
to stoop to a French maid get-up

so you pull the black lace dress
over cross-straps of the demi's
fair-ground & robe your arms
in velvet gloves & extend your Irish
into a black pair of 'Semi-Sheer/Night-Sky'

you top the flapper's ensemble with baby-pearl,
overlong, in triple-strands as a colleague helps
with the shoe-bows, improvising, proud
of the ensemble but drained from drawing humor
for the face of the day--

you head uptown to the masque
& I'm en route, south, passing brown
Bronx tenements lit up by holiday fire
wary of winter & insiders gearing to go right
& crown the first George king

I feel a city drop expensive karma,
I pass under the fusillade of blues
& the orange & black streamers;

I wander & wait for connections
that never come: I realize words are only articulated
idiocy without the mouthpiece-safety of a mask
to broadcast truths that will scatter the self—

I chat with bouncers disguised as queens
I meet Shakespeare's Helena roiling Puritans
& a mob attorney who hugs a lovely harlequin;
I applaud a Laotian couple dressed as rainbowfish
and a Haitian stud asks me, *doc', can you please modify
the botched surgery on these Aunt Jemima tits of mine?*

Then a friend unrolls red carpet toward you, for me
& I walk the path: am I a resurgent Orpheus, facing
Eurydice, found, safe, in a stanza she's never left?

you welcome me to the dreamer's dream

I give you a hand to mind: a dance, in fact,
as if our meeting is a Samhain prophecy
a song of action, sent to us from the centuries,
the ancestors emblazoned in overhead strobes;

for you I could marry word to color:
red-magic to your lips; sun & tidal
green to your eyes & morning-dove-
in-white, up & down your skin

this is how one 'gets the touch' & though staying,
one goes from here to a better-there—
I listen as a way of making love of you—
you're encouraging of everyone's desires;
you underscore it with your gentle take it
or leave it acceptance of the universe—*as is*
& *as in* "why-not-take a handful of stars
& hold them in the palm, the ornaments
or earrings, before restoring them to the galaxy
& smiling shyly, like a shopper, sated by the trying?"

night empties itself of black & its vacancy is
more than we can with-stand, so we head home,
down boulevards & avenues of moon-rock;

I escort you to a brick house
across from the train-yard's
barbed wire where weeds
struggle to live in the chill
& pre-dawn birds get busy
with invisible trills.

you say phoning you is one thing but
believing that impulse & knowing how
requires faith, ink & a reliable surface for writing,
so I fetch a book of poems from the back-seat—
& on the frontispiece I scribble your name
& number, work & home, separate, in digits
& on its vowels, I mark accomplishments
I'll happily die having achieved

why do we always live very far from the letters
of our young lives? as I grew, so you grew,
you into me & me to you, too much room for *us*

we passed from the emerald ring in five years
to the gold & ivory, for another five & from a river-hill
we overtook the tenderness of ceremony
for a literal blistering & the hard travel

ten years later, waking without words we needed
& we were gone, like a masque that never was.

these days, when God
gets the better of me
I pull down that book of poems
& bypass the saccharine odes
& remember you by studying the frontispiece
the sloppy calligraphy of your number that night

sleeping alone, silently surfacing bliss,
I study verse below each page
your number & your name & ideograms
of a single life & its after-images of you

so let's read together what
the heart alone won't know

leave the old inscriptions, lost in time,
as new grass grows on ancient ramparts,

I am bound on a journey without end
& can no longer bear the song of the cuckoo.

Tim Keane was born and raised in New York City. His writing has earned awards from The National Endowment for the Arts and The Bronx Council on the Arts, and his poems, stories, translations and essays have been published internationally. He teaches writing and comparative literature at John Jay College of Criminal Justice in New York.